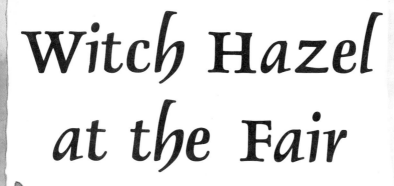

Witch Hazel at the Fair

E. Larreula R. Capdevila A. Wilkinson

Cambridge University Press

Cambridge New York Port Chester Melbourne Sydney

My name is Witch Hazel and, let me tell you, winters can be very boring – even for us witches. There aren't enough toads or lizards around to make a decent stew. And, as for magic, my spells seem to ice up before I get started.

But when I was much younger winters were *never* boring. I'll always remember that winter night long ago when an airmail letter arrived by bat-post.

I asked my dearest friend and companion, Goggletoot the owl, to read it to me. Not that I can't read, mind you, but owls have such good eyesight, don't they?

He said it was an invitation from my cousin Olive to a special fair in her village. There would be fun and games from dawn till dusk. I was so excited that I even warmed up a bit of magic to help me pack.

*'Stockings, knickers and jumper blue,
Get in the bag, you're coming too!'*

As soon as we were ready, we set off on my zoom-broom. I couldn't wait to get there! 'Goggletoot,' I said, 'there's nothing I like better than fun and games, as long as I'm the winner, of course. A little magic here and there to help me win . . . hee, hee! And why not?'

'Because that's cheating,' said Goggletoot.
What nonsense owls talk. Whoever said owls
were wise? They're just spoilsports.

Soon we were flying in over the village.
I spotted Cousin Olive waving at me
from the village square. Everyone
seemed delighted to see me.

Olive and I spent a very pleasant evening at her home. As we smartened up our clothes for the fair, she told me all about the other witches, wizards and ghosts who would be coming.

At midnight the fair began! While the village people lay fast asleep, we moonlighters danced the night away until dawn.

Goggletoot got rather bored. He said he didn't like dancing and anyway he had something better to do . . .

He went and joined the baby ghosts for their party – a breakfast of snake rolls and bowls of hot chocolate. He went in disguise, but I'm sure they must have noticed.

We were hot and thirsty after all our dancing, so we sat down for a glass of cool moon-dew syrup. The older wizards, those over two hundred years old, got down to a game of bowls. Still, I kept wondering when the real fun was going to start.

Next it was dancing in pairs. I danced with a
handsome young wizard who swept me off my feet in
a spell-binding waltz.

Goggletoot seized the microphone and
sang very tunefully, as owls do. He really
got the party off to a swinging start.

Suddenly the loudspeaker announced that the sack race was about to start. I couldn't use magic to help me because the other witches would have heard. So I had to think of another plan quickly! I tied springs to my feet!

Whoooo . . oops! I sprang so high that
I flew right over the winning flag
instead of going past it. Just my luck!

That made me all the more
determined to win the next race –
the broomstick race. Just before
the starter pistol went 'pop', I
tied a booster rocket to my
zoom-broom. I always keep a
spare booster in case my magic
broom dust runs out. With the
two together, I'd go twice as fast!

Wooosh! The booster rocket
went off with such a roar and a
sizzle that I was up and away
before the others had even got
off the ground!

I didn't see the winning flag at all this time! The booster rocket was so powerful that it whizzed me right round the earth twice. And I was beginning to wonder if I would ever come down . . .

At last I made a rather sudden
crash-landing. Unfortunately I
had missed all the other races!
There were the winners standing
on the platform with their prizes.
'Botheration!' After trying so
hard, I still hadn't won anything.
I thought Goggletoot looked
pretty miserable too.

However, I soon recovered when I heard that there was to be a beauty contest next. Well, as you can see, *this* was something I was sure I could win without . . . er . . . any help.

We all stood in line wearing our numbers while the judges made up their minds who was the most beautiful. Then they announced the winner. And, do you know, every single judge, even Goggletoot, chose *me*!

I was overjoyed as you can imagine! The
wizards crowded round my throne cheering
and singing.

Hoorah for Hazel the beauty queen!
Her cheeks have such a rosy sheen!
Her nose is as long as a garden hose.
She's a creature of beauty from head to toes!

They clapped and waved until I was quite dizzy
from it all. I can't understand why, but Cousin
Olive never did invite me to another fair.

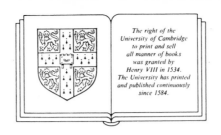

Published by the Press Syndicate of the University of Cambridge
The Pitt Building, Trumpington Street, Cambridge CB2 1RP
40 West 20th Street, New York, NY 10011, USA
10 Stamford Road, Oakleigh, Melbourne 3166, Australia

Originally published in Spanish 1988 as *La Fiesta Mayor de la Bruja Aburrida*
by Editorial Ariel S.A., Barcelona
© 1987 Editorial Ariel S.A.
First published in English by Cambridge University Press 1989 as *Witch Hazel at the Fair*.
English edition © Cambridge University Press 1989

Printed in Spain

British Library cataloguing-in-publication data
Larreula, E.
Witch Hazel at the Fair.
I. Title   II. Capdevila, R.   III. Wilkinson, A.
IV. La Fiesta Mayor de la Bruja Aburrida. *English*
863′.64 [J]

ISBN 0 521 37356 5